DATE DUE

Demco

LAKE OSWEGO JR. HIGH SCHOOL
2500 SW COUNTRY CLUB RD
LAKE OSWEGO, OR 97034
503-534-2335

LEADERS OF THE
MIDDLE AGES™

JOAN OF ARC Heroine of France

LEADERS OF THE
MIDDLE AGES™

JOAN OF ARC Heroine of
France

David Hilliam

rosen
central™

The Rosen Publishing Group, Inc., New York

Published in 2005 by The Rosen Publishing Group, Inc.
29 East 21st Street, New York, NY 10010

Library of Congress Cataloging-in-Publication Data

Hilliam, David.
Joan of Arc : heroine of France / David Hilliam. — 1st ed.
    p. cm. — (Leaders of the Middle Ages)
Summary: A discussion of the life and times of the French heroine, Joan of Arc, with illustrations from the medieval period.
Includes bibliographical references and index.
ISBN 1-4042-0164-5 (library binding)
1. Joan, of Arc, Saint, 1412–1431. 2. Christian women saints—France—Biography. 3. France—History—Charles VII, 1422–1461. [1. Joan, of Arc, Saint, 1412–1431. 2. Saints. 3. Women—Biography. 4. France—History—Charles VII, 1422–1461.]
I. Title. II. Series.
DC103.H478 2004
944'.026'092—dc22

                                                          2003021805

Manufactured in the United States of America

On the cover: A portrait of Joan of Arc, dated 1420. Background: An illuminated manuscript page showing the Hundred Years' War (1339–1453).

CONTENTS

LAND AT THE TIME OF JOAN OF ARC

SCOTLAND

IRELAND

WALES

ENGLAND

London

ENGLISH CHANNEL

Calais

Agincourt

Rouen

Reims

Paris

Orléans

Bourges

FRANCE

Poitiers

Bordeaux

GERMANY

ITALY

Rome

SPAIN

MEDITERRANEAN SEA

AFRICA

INTRODUCTION: JOAN OF ARC— HEROINE OF FRANCE

It is unlikely that any historian or biographer will ever have a complete understanding of the life of Joan of Arc. No one compares with her at any period of time or in any country.

Her story is that of a girl who had strange religious experiences and then stuck to her own beliefs about them, despite the Catholic Church's attempt to persuade her that she was being deceived by the devil. She defied the bishops and priests. She refused to take advice from high-ranking leaders in both the church and army, and she endured terrible punishment. But never once did she deny her deeply held personal beliefs in God. However, in order to try to understand her story, it's helpful to know about some beliefs and attitudes in medieval Europe.

This is an equestrian statue featuring Joan of Arc on a horse in Paris. The statue dates from 1899. Works of art that focus on the horse (with or without a rider) are known as equine art. A sculpture, statue, or other image of a person riding a horse—usually a military leader or king or queen—is referred to as equestrian art.

At that time, the teachings of the Catholic Church, led by the pope in Rome, dominated everyone's lives. At the front of people's minds was the hope of going to heaven or the fear of going to hell. One could be saved from hell by doing good deeds, avoiding sexual relationships outside marriage, and accepting the beliefs of the church that were taught by the priests. Salvation (to be saved from hell and to go to heaven when you died) was the most important goal in life.

On the other hand, damnation meant going to hell after you died and being tortured there forever. It was firmly believed that the devil was constantly trying to tempt people into sin and keep their souls away from God. Pictures and carvings of good people going to heaven and sinners going to hell are found in medieval churches throughout Europe.

Bishops and priests held an extremely important role in helping people avoid damnation. They gave advice, heard people confess their sins, and pardoned them if they were truly sorry. The worst sin of all was pride. This occurred when an individual was so convinced of being right that he or she defied the priests and insisted that his or her interpretation of ideas and events was true.

It is within this context that Joan of Arc's story takes place. Aside from her legendary courage, she

This is an image of a High Mass from an illuminated manuscript called the *Berry Book of Hours.* Such richly illustrated books were commissioned by wealthy individuals. The Duke of Berry commissioned this work. The images provide insight into life in the late fourteenth and early fifteenth centuries in France.

is remarkable for being an outstanding military commander. This aspect of her life was summed up by Mark Twain, the author of "Saint Joan of Arc: Part IV," from *What Is Man? and Other Essays of Mark Twain:*

> There is no one to compare her with, no one to measure her by. There have been other young generals, but they were not girls; young generals, but they have been soldiers before they were generals; she began as a general; she commanded the first army she ever saw; she led it from victory to victory, and never lost a battle with it; there have been young commanders-in-chief, but none so young as she; she is the only soldier in history who has held the supreme command of a nation's armies at the age of seventeen.

With such a record, it's not surprising that Joan of Arc is remembered with such pride. Aside from being the greatest national heroine of France, her name is a reminder to all to stand up for what you believe in.

JOAN'S EARLY CHILDHOOD

Joan of Arc (Jeanne d'Arc in French) was born in 1412 in the little village of Domrémy, near the town of Vaucouleurs in eastern France. Her parents were Jacques d'Arc and Isabelette. At the time of Joan's birth, France was not a united country as it is today. Instead, it was divided into separate provinces. Joan was born in the province of Lorraine, which was ruled by a duke.

Joan's parents were respectable peasant farmers. They were not desperately poor, but they were certainly humble and hardworking. Joan herself, the youngest of a family of five, led the life of a girl typical of the times. She was not given any formal education and she couldn't read or write. Nevertheless, she was proud of her sewing and spinning. In fact, she boasted that she could beat almost any woman in these practical skills. As was

This house in Domrémy is the actual birthplace of Joan of Arc. The house has become a popular shrine for tourists and history lovers. Next to it is a museum devoted to Joan of Arc. The house has been restored.

normal for the times, she busied herself with house-work at home. When needed, she would help out on the farm by looking after the animals in the fields and occasionally doing some of the plowing. Joan, who was a tough young teenager, was quite able to handle a plow.

Everyone who knew her spoke of her devoted love of the church and her desire to help those who were sick or poor. Her friends and neighbors were impressed with her devout way of life. She often went alone into her village church to pray.

Sometimes she was even teased for it. A lot of the information that is known about Joan's life was written in the 1962 book *Joan of Arc*, by French writer and historian Régine Pernoud. Pernoud's book documents the trial records of Joan. Pernoud's book is the source used for the trial records quoted in a later chapter of this book. According to Pernoud, Joan's next-door neighbor said, "She was so good, simple and pious that I and the other young girls would tell her that she was too pious."

Joan also enjoyed taking part in local games and customs with other girls of the village. Apparently, near Domrémy, there was a tree associated with ancient folklore, called the Fairies' Tree. This tree was thought to be magic. It grew near a miraculous spring. The girls would decorate the tree with garlands and sometimes dance and sing around it. On one special day, called Springs' Sunday (*dimanche des fontaines* in French), boys and girls would gather there and have a picnic. They would eat their bread and drink the magical spring water.

These peasant women are harvesting grain in an illustration from the *Berry Book of Hours* (in French, *Les Trés Riches Heures du Duc de Berry*). The Duke of Berry, who commissioned this devotional book (private prayer book), was the brother of King Charles V.

Meanwhile, there was a young man who was eager to marry Joan. There was no obvious reason why the two shouldn't have married. However, to her parents' great surprise, Joan was not at all interested. The young man himself actually took her to court in the nearby town of Toul for breach of promise. But, as young Joan (who at this time was just sixteen) had made no such promise to marry him, the court decided in her favor.

Although no one was aware of it at the time, the main reason Joan had turned him down was a secret only she knew. In fact, it was a most extraordinary secret. Joan had been hearing voices and having visions for several years, ever since she was thirteen. The first occurrance must have been alarming for a young peasant girl. One summer's day around noon, she suddenly heard a strange voice and saw a bright light. By her own account, she was very frightened. But after she had heard the voice three times, she had a firm conviction that it was St. Michael who was speaking to her.

When questioned about this later, she explained under oath that she "saw" him several times before knowing for certain that it was St. Michael. Then she learned from him that St. Catherine and St. Margaret would also soon visit her. St. Michael told her that she must do what the saints instructed her to do and that she would be guided by them. Joan was to believe everything they said, and she was to accept that all this was according to God's orders.

JOAN IS ORDERED TO SEE THE KING

At first, the voices only spoke of the need to behave properly and go to church regularly. But then, "twice or thrice [three times] a week," according to Joan, for months and years on end, she was given astonishing and specific instructions. She was told that she should leave home, go to central France (in other words, leave her native province of Lorraine), and relieve the siege of Orléans (a city being besieged by the English army). The voices also told her to go to the aid of the king of France. At that time, he was living in the famous castle of Chinon, near the Loire valley.

The king was known as the Dauphin because of his heraldic emblem of a dolphin (the French for "dolphin" is *dauphin*). Furthermore, as the Dauphin still needed to be crowned, Joan's voices told her that "God Almighty" would guide her in leading the king to his coronation at Reims Cathedral. It was here that kings of France were traditionally crowned. A further instruction was that her father should know nothing of all of this.

This photograph shows part of the famous cathedral in Reims. It is known as the cathedral of Notre-Dame at Reims. It is located on the Vesle River northeast of Paris. The cathedral was the site of twenty-five coronations of French kings. These included the crowning of Louis VIII in 1223, Charles X in 1825, and Charles VII in 1429 in the presence of Joan of Arc.

Throughout the time when Joan was hearing these voices, she said nothing about them to her parents, family, or friends. At last, St. Catherine and St. Margaret told her that she should leave Domrémy and go to speak to Robert de Baudricourt. He was the captain in charge of the castle at Vaucouleurs. Once there, she was to explain her mission of leading the king's army to victory against the English forces who had invaded France.

Of course, this would be difficult for Joan. It meant that she would have to leave home without making her parents suspicious. She would later explain that she didn't like deceiving them, but God had commanded it. As a part of her plan, she asked if she could stay with her uncle for a few days. He lived a few miles away from their home. Once she arrived there, she explained her situation to him and persuaded him to take her to Robert de Baudricourt. She also talked him into telling her parents that she was helping her aunt, who happened to be expecting a baby at that time.

Joan's first attempt to see Robert de Baudricourt, in May 1428, was a disaster. Boldly, she told him that God had sent her to him to ask his help in going to see the Dauphin. She also stated that she was to lead the French army and take the Dauphin to Reims to be crowned. All this seemed like pure nonsense to de Baudricourt. He sent her away without a moment's hesitation, telling her uncle to smack her ears so that she should learn better sense. It's not recorded what her parents thought when she got back home. However, they must have realized that Joan was having some strange ideas.

Early the following year, 1429, Joan got her uncle to take her to see de Baudricourt a second time. This time she had her parents' permission. Once again, he refused to take her seriously. Surprisingly, this didn't upset Joan in the least. She said that her voices had always told her this would happen. She spent several weeks with her uncle and aunt, and ultimately everyone knew of her intentions. She made friends with Jean de Metz and Bertrand de Poulengy, some of de Baudricourt's own officers. She inspired them with her own enthusiasm to lead an army against the English. Then, from Vaucouleurs, she set off by herself to see the Duke of Lorraine. She impressed him so much that he gave her a horse and some money.

By now, the inhabitants of Vaucouleurs were intrigued with the whole situation. They came up with a helpful plan. Joan, who believed that God was commanding her to dress like a man, was outfitted in men's clothing. Her uncle and a friend of his generously gave her a better horse. With all this help, Joan saw de Baudricourt for the third time. Aside from being fully prepared to go to the Dauphin, she also was supported by a number of trustworthy companions. Her burning sincerity and conviction had persuaded them to join her in leading an army against the English.

Because she was so persistent, de Baudricourt gave in. He allowed her to set off on her extraordinary

This tapestry shows Joan of Arc and her armed escort riding toward the castle of Chinon.

mission, accompanied by an escort of eight of his own men, including de Metz and de Poulengy. They were to go to the castle of Chinon, where the Dauphin was staying. This was about 100 miles (160 kilometers) southwest of Orléans. However, before they left, de Baudricourt took the precaution of ordering a priest to examine her. This was to see if she really was inspired by God and not by the devil. Having gained the priest's approval, Joan and her companions set off. Before leaving,

BURGUNDY

One of the most important provinces of France was Burgundy, which is located in the east. During Joan of Arc's lifetime, the Duke of Burgundy had joined forces with the English and was therefore an enemy of the king of France. Burgundians posed a serious threat to anyone who continued to support the Dauphin. Joan's village of Domrémy was close to Lorraine's border with Burgundy.

During the Middle Ages, France was divided into many provinces, each ruled by a duke or count. These leaders were independent, but in theory they held allegiance to the king of France. France itself was a relatively small area around Paris.

Joan cut her hair short. This way, she looked even more like a man.

Their eleven-day journey to see the Dauphin would be extremely dangerous. The route was occupied by English soldiers and Burgundians who were allies of the English. Joan's group found it safer to

travel by night. Regardless of all the danger, Joan showed herself to be quite fearless as they moved through hostile territory. In fact, her courage was infectious. In later years, her companions spoke of her radiant self-confidence and goodness, how she never swore, and how she constantly made the sign of the cross when she said her prayers. She told them to have no fear. By the time they reached Chinon, they were all convinced that she *was* sent by God.

In March 1429, Joan arrived to meet the Dauphin, future King Charles VII of France. It was an extraordinary meeting, with astonishing results. However, before we can understand what happened at Chinon, it's important to know something of the history that led up to this event, especially the tense relationship between France and England.

This illustration is from a fifteenth-century French manuscript that tells the life of Joan of Arc. In this image, a messenger is being received by the king and his council.

FRANCE AND ENGLAND: THE HISTORICAL BACKGROUND

Throughout the Middle Ages, relations between France and England were complicated. The crucial starting point was the year 1066—the most famous date in English history. This was when Duke William of Normandy crossed the English Channel with his Norman army and defeated King Harold, the last king of the Saxons.

As a result of his victory, Duke William had himself crowned as King William I of England. Afterward he came to be known as William the Conqueror. However, he still had his land possessions in Normandy, so his territories straddled the English Channel. From then on, all the subsequent kings of England laid claim to various parts of France. Sometimes, because of marriage, the English kings owned and ruled more of France than the reigning French kings.

This is a copy of an anonymous portrait of Edward III. Edward was born on November 13, 1312, at Windsor Castle in Berkshire, England. He was crowned king on January 25, 1327, at the famed Westminster Abbey. After a fifty-year reign as king, he died on June 21, 1377, at Sheen Palace in Surrey.

Henry II, for example, added the huge province of Aquitaine (in southern France) to his empire. He did this when he married its ruler, the wealthy Duchess of Aquitaine, in 1152.

Through warfare, over the next 150 years, French kings regained much of the land in France that England had once claimed as its own. Therefore, in 1327, when a fourteen-year-old boy, Edward III, became king of England, only the southwestern provinces of Gascony and Guienne remained in English hands. Because these were important wine-producing areas, the young king was determined to hold on to these territories and possibly expand them.

EDWARD III AND THE HUNDRED YEARS' WAR

Edward III was a remarkably strong and capable young man, who enjoyed the thrill of battles. Since his mother had been a French princess, he calculated that he had a stronger claim to the French throne than the French king Philip VI. He argued that Philip was only a cousin of the previous French king, whereas he, Edward, was a nephew. There were lengthy legal arguments that led nowhere. The French upheld what was known as the Salic Law. This law banned inheritance through a female line, thus excluding Edward's mother's claim to the throne.

The result was that, in 1337, King Edward III boldly declared war on France. And so began what historians now call the Hundred Years' War. This did not mean that battles raged constantly for a hundred years. Rather, off and on throughout that period, the French and English were always ready to

This is a page from a French illuminated manuscript that illustrates the *Chronicles of Jean Froissart*. Jean Froissart (1333–1404) was a poet and historian. His chronicles are necessary to understand fourteenth-century Europe, especially the events of the Hundred Years' War.

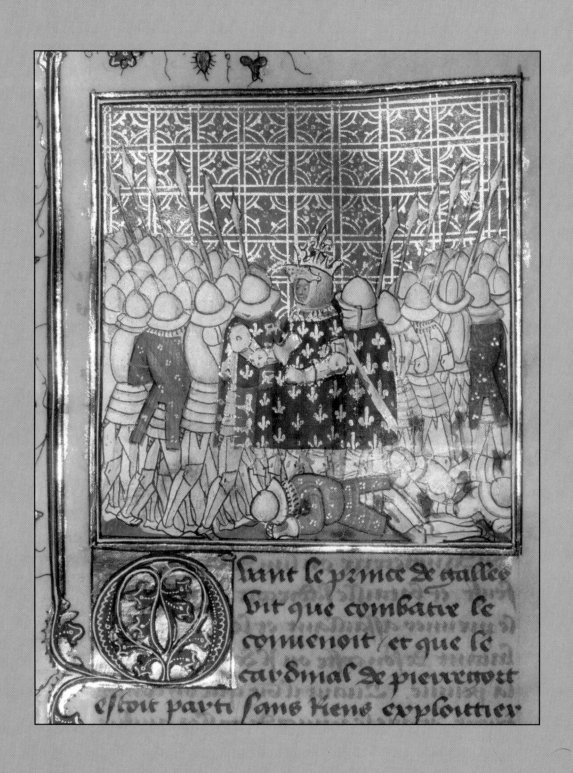

quant le prince de galles
vit que combatre le
commenoit / et que le
cardinal de pierregort
estoit parti sans riens exploittier

fight each other. These battles took place both at sea and on land.

In 1340, Edward III had his first victory, a sea battle off what is now the Belgian coast. During this battle, he almost completely destroyed the French fleet. In 1346, he followed this up with a major battle at Crécy in northern France. He then marched north and laid siege to the port of Calais. After a bitter winter, Calais surrendered to him. Ten years later, in 1356, Edward's son, the fearsome Black Prince, won an equally impressive battle against the French at Poitiers.

After this, the two sides signed a peace treaty. According to the treaty, Edward gave up his claim to the French throne in return for Calais and a large area in northern France. The treaty also meant that his lands in southwestern France were greatly increased. At this point, Edward now controlled about a third of the country.

Toward the end of Edward's reign, a new French commander, Bertrand du Guesclin, began to win back much of the ground gained by the English. The Black Prince became sick and died. Then, Edward III died in 1377. After this, English possessions in France dwindled to just a few coastal towns such as Bordeaux and Calais and their surrounding areas.

This illuminated manuscript illustrates Henry of Monmouth (the future King Henry V) being knighted by King Richard II. Henry is on horseback on the far left. King Henry V was born on September 16, 1387, at Monmouth Castle. Monmouth is a 2,000-year-old town that at one point was a Roman settlement.

The next two English kings were neither able nor willing to continue the struggles in France. It wasn't until 1413 that England once again found itself led by a warrior king—the famous Henry V.

Tall, handsome, young, and strong, he was a charismatic military leader, as portrayed in William Shakespeare's play *Henry V*. Even more important, he was desperately anxious to carry on the wars in France where his great-grandfather Edward III had left off.

This image shows a scene from the Battle of Agincourt. At Agincourt, the English, under Henry V, won an overwhelming victory over the French.

HENRY V AND THE ENGLISH VICTORY AT AGINCOURT

Almost as soon as he came to the English throne, Henry claimed to be the rightful king of France. He started making preparations to invade the country. Once again, the French brought out the old Salic Law arguments for discussion. However, Henry brushed these aside with impatience. Two years later, in 1415, Henry fought and won what was certainly one of the greatest battles in English history, the Battle of Agincourt, in northern France.

For the French, the battle was a total disaster. The terrible news of defeat shot through their country like a thunderbolt. The villagers of Domrémy in eastern Burgundy must have been sad to hear the news. Joan of Arc's family would surely have shared in the mood of the moment. Little Joan was only three at the time.

While England celebrated Henry's victory, the French were suffering under the rule of Charles VI, or Charles the Mad, as he was called. During his very long reign, his kingdom was split into many parts. Almost all of northern France and the western provinces of Guienne and Gascony were held by the English. A large part of eastern France and most of Flanders were ruled by the Duke of Burgundy (who was an ally of the English). Brittany was ruled by an independent duke. The territory ruled by Charles the Mad was in the south. This added up to less than half of France.

Then, in 1422, everything changed. Quite unpredictably, both the king of France, Charles the Mad, and the king of England, Henry V—the victor of Agincourt—died. The heir to the throne of England was a nine-month-old baby, Henry VI.

Because he was so young, there had to be a regent (someone with the authority to act as king

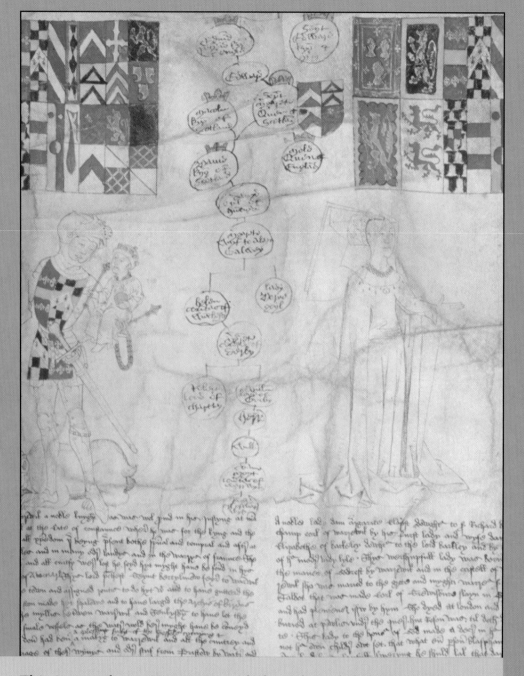

This image shows Henry VI as a baby *(above left)* being held by the Earl of Warwick. Henry VI, who was born on December 6, 1421, was the only child of Henry V and Catherine of Valois. He married Margaret of Anjou in 1445. They had one son, Edward, who was later killed in battle. Henry came to the throne as a young boy after the early death of his father.

until young Henry VI grew up). Henry V's younger brother, John, Duke of Bedford, who was married to Anne of Burgundy, was appointed as regent. He was expected to carry on the war in France.

The heir to the throne of France, the son of Charles the Mad, was Charles VII. He was known as the Dauphin, the traditional title of the eldest son of the French king.

In 1422, the nineteen-year-old Dauphin was theoretically king of France. Unfortunately, however, his kingdom was in a sorry state. Furthermore, according to the Treaty of Troyes (made after the Battle of Agincourt), Henry V had become the heir to the throne. Now it was possible to argue that Henry V's successor, the baby king of England, was the rightful king of France.

All this confusion was made worse by the fact that Paris, the Dauphin's capital city, was in the hands of the English. As well, Reims, the traditional place where the kings of France held their coronation, was held by the English. This meant that poor young Charles couldn't even be crowned.

Six years later, when Joan of Arc set out from Vaucouleurs to meet the Dauphin, the situation was getting very serious for the French. The Dauphin, then twenty-six and still uncrowned, was thin, pale,

Pour lan mil. cccc. et sept.
Coment le duc dorleans eut par
lottroy du roy son frere la duche dac
quitame. Et lors furent fautes treues
entre le royaulme de france et dangle
terre. Chappitre. xxiiii.

and very unsure of himself. People sneeringly referred to him as king of Bourges, the city where he had his headquarters. Meanwhile, the powerful and warlike Duke of Bedford, who was virtually the king of England since Henry VI was still a child, was pushing his armies farther south. He had surrounded the key city of Orléans and was keeping it under siege. When it fell, this would be the signal for him to make a final major attack on the Dauphin's territory in the south of France.

It seemed a desperately hopeless situation for the Dauphin. But who could foresee the effect an unknown seventeen-year-old girl would have on his situation. In February 1429, Joan of Arc arrived with a few companions at the Dauphin's castle at Chinon, urgently demanding to see him.

This illuminated manuscript page illustrates Charles VI of France and Henry V of England signing the Treaty of Troyes on May 21, 1420. The treaty meant that Henry would become heir to the throne of France. Henry was also to marry Charles's daughter, Catherine of Valois. At the time, Catherine was eighteen years old and very beautiful.

JOAN MEETS THE DAUPHIN

After their eleven-day journey to Chinon, Joan and her companions reached the nearby town of Sainte Catherine de Fierbois. From there, she sent a message to the Dauphin that she wanted to see him. At about noon on February 23, 1429, she arrived at Chinon and stayed at an inn. She and her companions had a meal, and in the evening, they went up to the castle. They hoped to be received by Charles.

At first, the Dauphin was somewhat reluctant to see her. However, after some discussion with his advisers, he decided to allow her to visit him. Curiosity must have played a major part in this decision. He was probably curious to see her and to hear what this unusual peasant girl dressed as a young man could possibly wish to say to him.

The Dauphin must have been utterly amazed at what Joan said. According to Jean Pasquerel, her confessor and companion on all her campaigns, the Count of Vendôme led her to the Dauphin, who asked Joan her name and why she had come to see him. Her reply (as told in Pernoud's *Joan of Arc*) was bold and direct. Jean Pasquerel quoted her exact words in later years:

> "Gentle Dauphin," she replied, "Joan the Maid is my name, and to you is sent word by me from the King of Heaven that you will be anointed [have holy oil ceremonially poured over one's head] and crowned in the town of Reims and you will be Lieutenant to the King of Heaven who is King of France."

The Dauphin was obviously astonished by this and asked her a number of questions. Then Joan continued:

> "I tell thee, on behalf of God, that thou art true heir of France and king's son, and He has sent me to thee to lead thee to Reims, that thou mayst receive thy coronation and thy consecration."

This is the audience room (meeting room) in the castle of Chinon where Joan of Arc first met with the Dauphin.

"Consecration" is another word for anointing. It was believed that a king received a special blessing from God when he had holy oil poured over his head.

It's important to realize that the Dauphin himself had always had doubts about his own legitimacy. He seriously questioned whether he was truly entitled to become king. Therefore, when Joan hailed him in the name of God with the words "thou art true heir of France," he must have begun to feel a tremendous amount of self-confidence.

After this, Joan spoke alone with the Dauphin. She told him a secret that only the Dauphin himself knew. There was no way that Joan could have possibly known this secret on her own. This revelation came as a considerable shock to the Dauphin. Nonetheless, it reassured him that Joan *did* have access to godly powers. It is not entirely certain what occurred between them. But many years later, one of Charles's closest courtiers reportedly revealed that Joan had quoted to the Dauphin his most secret personal daily prayer. The result was that it led the Dauphin to view her with deep respect.

JOAN IS EXAMINED AND INTERROGATED

The Dauphin sent Joan to Poitiers to be examined to be doubly sure that she was taken seriously and that her powers really did come from God and not the devil. She met with some of the most learned and respected professors, bishops, and theologians in the country. This included the archbishop of Reims, who was then chancellor of France.

They asked Joan why they should believe her. Then they suggested that if God really wanted to help them get rid of their English enemies, he wouldn't need soldiers. She replied that soldiers would be the means by which God would do his work. Next, they asked her whether she could give them further proof of the truth of what she was saying. Joan responded by saying that proof would come as she fulfilled the promises God was making. Joan listed four specific things that would happen.

First, she prophesied that she would defeat the English (who were besieging the city of Orléans) and liberate the people of Orléans. Second, she would take the Dauphin to be crowned at Reims. Third, she prophesied that the city of Paris would be freed from the occupying English forces. Finally, she said that the Duke of Orléans, who was at that time held captive in the Tower of London, would return to France.

These interrogations lasted for three weeks. It says much for Joan's strong personality that she survived the questionings. Despite their obvious initial doubts, by the end of their examination the interrogators were convinced that she *was* truly inspired by God. Everyone recognized that her trust in God was genuine. But even then, as a final precaution, the interrogators asked two ladies of the Dauphin's court to examine her physically to make sure she really was a girl and a virgin. In medieval times, virginity was very important. It proved purity and goodness.

This final test was done under the supervision of Yolande of Aragon, the king's mother-in-law. Joan passed this final test with no problems.

JOAN IS EQUIPPED FOR WAR

This illustration, circa 1420, shows Joan of Arc in armor. She is holding a sword and carrying a standard decorated with a fleur-de-lys.

At last, after all this, the Dauphin believed it was safe to trust Joan and to allow her to carry out her extraordinary mission. He ordered that she be escorted to the city of Tours, where she would be equipped with a special coat of white armor and provided with three personal flags: a long standard, a smaller square banner, and a small triangular pennant.

Every army captain had attendants and standard bearers because, once encased in armor, they needed a distinguishing flag to identify who they were. Joan herself would carry the standard and one of her attendants would carry the pennant. This would indicate her exact location on the battlefield.

The larger banner had an image of Christ crucified. Joan used it to rally her troops and priests for prayer meetings in the days before battle. She ordered

43

all the priests who were accompanying them as army chaplains to assemble twice a day. In the morning and evening, they would pray and sing hymns to the Virgin Mary. She was believed to be the most important saint in heaven. The soldiers were also urged to attend these assemblies, but they weren't allowed to join until they had confessed their sins. Only the pure and holy were to be part of Joan's army.

The large standard, which Joan needed to carry into battle, was white. It was decorated with embroidered pictures of fleurs-de-lys (lilies), with two angels at the sides, and the names of Jesus and Mary embroidered in silk.

Joan also needed a sword. She claimed that her voices had told her exactly where she could find one. They had said she would find it behind the altar in the church of the little village of Sainte Catherine de Fierbois. When she sent someone to look for it, the sword was hidden in the ground and was quite rusty. Nevertheless, it was easily cleaned up. Joan knew it was the sword described by her voices because it had five crosses engraved on it. She begged the priests of the church to allow her to keep it, and they agreed. They even gave her a sheath to go with it.

Eventually, after the three-week examination at Poitiers and after she had properly equipped herself

This illuminated manuscript image from the *Bedford Book of Hours* illustrates typical peasant life, which was similar to the life that Joan and her family lived. At left, a man threshes grain. At right, a female figure represents the star sign Virgo. It's fascinating to contrast where Joan of Arc came from with what she became— a powerful leader.

for war, Joan was ready to do battle with the English at the siege of Orléans. She was not put in full charge of the army. Control of operations was in the hands of the Duke of Alençon. The young duke and soldier was a close friend of the Dauphin's. However, Joan, who had until recently been just a simple peasant girl, was now treated as a captain. At age seventeen, she was in command of her own company of men-at-arms. She could hardly wait to begin.

Raising the
Siege of Orléans

Joan's success in relieving the siege of Orléans in May 1429 is so extraordinary, it reads like fiction.

The city of Orléans is about 54 miles (104 km) south of Paris at the northernmost point of a huge sweeping bend of the river Loire. All the territory south of the river was held by the French and ruled by the uncrowned Dauphin. All the territory to the north was held by the English.

Ever since October 12, 1428, an English army led by Sir John Talbot had surrounded Orléans. The army was hoping that when they captured the city, the pathway to southern France would be clear. During this six-month siege, the people of Orléans suffered from lack of food. Occasionally, supplies could be smuggled in from the south, across the wide river. But this could only be done under the watchful eyes of the English, who were steadily tightening their stranglehold. The city itself was surrounded by a wall more than 29 feet (9 m) tall. It had twenty-four great towers built at intervals around it.

Joan set off on April 29, 1429, with the Dauphin's army of about 3,000 men from Blois, which is 35 miles (56 km) west of Orléans. She was accompanied by the Duke of Alençon; Étienne de Vignoles, or La Hire, who was thought to be the best

This is what is called a border illustration (a drawing in the margin) from the register of the Paris Parliament. It dates from 1428 to 1436. The page shows an image of Joan of Arc with her sword and banner on the left, and notes about the siege of Orléans on the right.

cavalry soldier in France; Gilles de Rais, known as Bluebeard; and several other high-ranking officers. These were all older, seasoned military men with years of fighting experience. As for Joan, she was a young country girl, who had never once taken part in any military operation.

With years of fighting experience, it was not surprising that, in their hearts, her older companions could hardly take Joan seriously. After all, she had no reputation for military skill. Her greatest strength was the burning conviction that her voices were guiding her to victory—specifically, that they were telling her to attack Orléans from the north. Joan didn't take much notice of the route they were taking, But when they arrived on the southern bank of the Loire and she saw the towers of Orléans lying northward, she was absolutely enraged. She realized that they had taken no notice of her plans and that they were treating her like a child.

She turned on them, shouting furiously that they had let her down and that her voices must be obeyed. At this moment, they were joined by the Bastard of Orléans (also known as Count Dunois). Dunois was the illegitimate half-brother of the king and commander of the defending forces of Orléans. He had daringly crossed the river to meet them. Joan turned on him, too. According to later records, Dunois himself testified that she asked him:

> Are you the Bastard of Orléans? And was it
> you who advised that I should come here,
> to this side of the river, and not go straight

to where Talbot is? In God's name! The Lord's advice is surer and wiser than yours.

It seems incredible for a peasant girl to be so self-confident and outspoken that she would address a royal commander like this. It may be that Dunois was rather amused by her. In fact, he didn't lose his temper, but merely pointed out the wisdom of being cautious. He also outlined his own plan of action. He had reason and experience on his side, and the

EAN · CONTE · DE · DVNOIS
AS TARD · D'ORLEANS · MORT · LAN · 14

An image of the Count Dunois, also known as the Bastard of Orléans. Dunois was born on April 18, 1403, and his proper name was Count Dunois, Jean d'Orléans). He was the son of Louis, Duke of Orléans, and Mariette d'Enghien. He was with Joan of Arc at Orléans, Jargeau, Meung, Beaugency, Patay, Reims, and Paris.

other commanders agreed with him. But Joan was not to be browbeaten. She insisted that she was right. "Wait a while," she said. "For in God's name all will enter the town."

Their immediate problem was the strong northeast wind. This was preventing boats from crossing the river to take the much-needed supplies into Orléans. But then, to everyone's amazement, even as Joan was speaking, the direction of the wind dramatically changed and came from the west. It seemed like a miracle. As a result, Count Dunois stated that he "believed in Joan as [he] had not before." After this remarkably sudden wind change, Joan increasingly took charge of the operations. Not surprisingly, her orders were accepted without question.

ACTION AT ORLÉANS

The following days were filled with action. Joan had previously dictated a letter to Sir John Talbot, calling on him in the name of God to surrender. Although it was written in astonishingly bold language, Talbot ignored it. After all, why should he pay attention to a letter coming from such a radical young woman? However, with so much gossip and speculation among the townsfolk, her presence and intention to relieve the siege could not be ignored.

The townsfolk of Orléans were thrilled when Joan made her appearance. She was dressed in white armor and rode a splendid white horse. There was a feeling of expectancy and hope as she inspected the

English strongholds encircling the town. These consisted of a series of fortifications known as bastilles.

The first victory of the siege came on Wednesday, May 4. It happened at the Bastille de St. Loup, a tower some way out of the city. The tower was occupied by the English and commanded by Talbot himself. Unknown to Joan, some

This photo shows the house where Joan of Arc stayed in Orléans from April 19 to May 9, 1429.

of her soldiers had gone there to provoke action. She was resting when, suddenly, her voices spoke up, telling her that fighting was in progress. Joan leapt from her bed, shouted to her page to help her get her armor on, and flung herself into the saddle. She dashed off to join the action, just managing to grab her standard as it was passed out to her through an upstairs window.

When Joan got to St. Loup, she was horrified to see her men in retreat. Their attack had been

These are the seals of three of Joan of Arc's well-respected troops: the Count of Dunois, Gilles de Rais, and Xaintrailles. Seals were used as a form of signature and also as a way to secure important documents from being read by the wrong person. To open a document, the seal would have to be broken.

half-hearted. The English had quickly responded with a successful counterattack. Instantly, she took charge of the situation. She forced her men to turn back to the offensive and personally led them to victory by taking St. Loup by storm. Talbot just managed to escape. However, hundreds of his English troops were slaughtered.

By now, everyone had complete trust in Joan and obeyed her instructions without question. She decreed that on the next day, Thursday, May 5, (which was Ascension Day), there would be no fighting, but all should make their confessions. This would purify them for fighting the following day.

JOAN ACHIEVES VICTORY AT ORLÉANS

On Friday, two more English fortresses were taken. These were the Bastille de St. Jean le Blanc and the fortified monastery of Les Augustins. Once again, Joan took the lead. She urged her men forward, even though at one time they had been panicking into a retreat. "In the name of God, forward!" she shouted. "Forward, boldly." Mesmerized by the sheer force of her personality, her soldiers turned back and fought their way to victory. Proudly, Joan set up her standard on the walls of the Augustine monastery.

Next, a pair of twin towers known as Les Tourelles had to be taken. Upon returning to base, however, she encountered opposition from the other commanders. In her absence, they had decided that there would be no more fighting until they had received reinforcements from Blois. Joan strongly disagreed with them all. She had more work than ever to do the next day, she said. However, she prophesied that blood would flow from her body "above [her] breast." She declared: "You have been with your council and I have been

MEDIEVAL ARMOR

Medieval armor was heavy and complicated. In the early Middle Ages, those who could afford it wore coats of chain mail. However, after about 1300, plate armor was used. This was often highly

decorated with engraving and covered the whole body. Because of the need for flexibility, there were many joints, so there were dozens of separate pieces. These were joined together by leather hinges. Each piece had a special name. The arrow that hit Joan might have gotten between these pieces of armor. Statues of Joan almost always show her wearing plate armor.

This image illustrates the Battle of Crécy, which took place in August 1346. Although the French had a larger army, the English won at Crécy because their archers were able to stop the French cavalry charge.

with mine. Believe me, my council will endure; yours will come to nothing!" Again, her extreme confidence won them over.

The next day, Saturday, May 7, they fought the decisive battle of Les Tourelles. Joan ordered her troops to begin the attack at seven in the morning. She herself was at the front. La Hire, one of the chief commanders, and many others who later gave clear accounts of what happened were also there. She was urging everyone forward as they brought their ladders to the base of the towers. Suddenly, she was hit by an arrow, just as she had foretold, between pieces of her armor.

An illustration of the siege of Orléans, one of the many battles in the famous Hundred Years' War. The very long siege of Orléans was conducted by the English. It was heroically ended by Joan of Arc on Sunday, May 8, 1429.

Joan cried out in pain and had to be taken away from the fighting for a while. The English yelled with delight. Her own troops were weary and dispirited, and Joan knew that she had to get back among them. Despite the pain and with great determination, she managed to pull out the head of the arrow. Joan got back on her horse and found that she could still ride. In spite of her wound, she grabbed her standard. As Joan always led from the front, the signal for her men to advance would be once she touched the wall with her standard. Accordingly, she set off, ordering that they "wait until the tail end of [her] standard touches the wall."

Joan got as far as the wall, and then her standard fluttered against it. A soldier yelled, "Look! It touches!" whereupon Joan shouted back, "Then enter! Everything is yours!" In the confusion, many English soldiers, including one of her chief opponents, Sir William Glasdale, fell into the river and drowned. Others surrendered. By then, Les Tourelles was in flames.

As dawn broke the next day, Joan and her men realized to their delight that the entire English army was in retreat. They had been unnerved by what they believed to be Joan's witchcraft. A superstitious rumor had gone around the English forces claiming that she was an evil witch. They had abandoned all their defenses, leaving their equipment and heavy guns behind.

On that Sunday, as Joan and her French army triumphantly entered Orléans, the scenes of hysterical joy among its citizens can hardly be described. French history has no parallel. For the people of Orléans, Joan was more than a successful military commander. Instead, she was a miraculous savior, sent from God.

THE CORONATION OF CHARLES VII IN REIMS CATHEDRAL

The victory at Orléans was the high point of Joan's military success. However, other victories would follow. She had proved herself to be a superb military commander. And her fearless way of leading the attacks led to one conclusion—that she really was divinely inspired, just as she always claimed to be. The citizens of Orléans regarded her victory as miraculous.

Having accomplished this first objective, she was now ready to turn to the next one: the crowning of the Dauphin in Reims Cathedral. It's necessary to understand the importance of coronations in medieval times. Everyone believed that kings received their authority from God by virtue of being anointed. An archbishop would perform the ceremony with holy oil. This anointing ceremony at a coronation gave

This illustration depicts Henry III's coronation. He is pictured holding a model of Westminster Abbey, which he rebuilt. The coronation took place on October 28, 1216. Every king and queen of England since William the Conqueror has been crowned in Westminster Abbey.

CROWNING AND ANOINTING

The crowning of kings is a very ancient ceremony. Any coronation service is extremely impressive. France no longer has a king, but England is still a monarchy. In England, the monarch is always crowned in Westminster Abbey. The kings of France were traditionally crowned in Reims Cathedral. There are two crucial moments in a coronation service. The first is when the archbishop pours some drops of holy oil over the new monarch. The second is the placing of a crown on the monarch's head. The act of anointing dates back to biblical times, when King Solomon was anointed by the prophet Nathan.

divine authority to the king. It was only after this that he could assume the special mystical power that properly belonged to kings.

Without question, Joan of Arc believed in the power of anointing. Unless the Dauphin was anointed and crowned, he would not be the true king. Furthermore, the traditional and proper place for the coronations of the kings of France was Reims Cathedral. However, the overriding difficulty for Joan and the Dauphin was that Reims was in the English-held area of northern France. She would have to fight her way to get there. This meant a treacherous journey through about 140 miles (225 km) of hostile territory. To make things even more difficult, even the city of Reims itself was in enemy hands.

JOAN PERSUADES THE DAUPHIN TO GO TO REIMS

Orléans was liberated on May 8, 1429. Three days later, Joan went to meet the Dauphin and persuade him to provide her with more troops. She needed to clear the Loire valley of the English and then push northeast to Reims, about 207 miles (129 km) east of Paris. However, this bold plan of action was against the advice of the Dauphin's military chiefs. They wanted to follow up the victory at Orléans, first by reconquering Normandy and then by recapturing Paris.

One of Joan's close fighting companions, Count Dunois, provided a fascinating account (mentioned in Pernoud's *Joan of Arc*) of how Joan overcame the chiefs' opposition to her passionate desire to go to Reims. He tells how Joan burst into the council chamber while the Dauphin was meeting with his advisers. Then she fell on her knees before him and embraced

This map, dated from 1645, shows an overview of the town of Reims. Like many medieval cities, Reims was protected by an impressive wall with gates that could be closed against an enemy attack.

his legs. "Noble Dauphin," she exclaimed, "don't keep on holding these long council meetings, but go to Reims as soon as possible, to receive the crown which you deserve!"

A bishop present at the meeting asked her to explain exactly how she received her inspiration. The Dauphin also urged her to give an explanation. First, Joan withdrew to pray for a short while. When she came back, she said that she had heard a voice that said to her, "Daughter of God, go, go, go. I shall be at your aid. Go!" She repeated these words, "Fille de Dieu, va, va, va" (daughter of God, go, go, go),

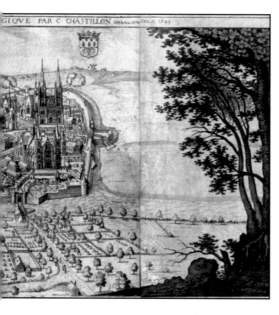

with her eyes raised to heaven. It seemed that no one could resist such divine power. She got her way.

ON THE WAY TO REIMS

By the beginning of June, Joan's army had been enlarged and re-equipped. Meanwhile, volunteers were flocking to join. It was still officially led by the Duke of Alençon. Fortunately for Joan, he was totally spellbound by her extraordinary self-confidence. He was easily guided by her enthusiasm. However, three towns in the Loire valley stood in their way before the final push to Reims: Jargeau, Meung, and Beaugency.

The speed of the Loire campaign was quite exceptional. On June 12, the army captured Jargeau; on June 15, it captured Meung; and on June 17, Beaugency fell. Then, one day later, on June 18, Joan's French forces fought a decisive battle at a little village called Patay. During this battle, the English lost more than 2,000 men. Meanwhile, only two men were killed from the armies of Joan and the Duke of Alençon. It was a humiliating defeat for the English. In addition, one of their important commanders, Sir John Talbot, was taken prisoner.

Joan played an important role in all these military engagements. Her courage was inspiring. For example, when Jargeau was taken, she was knocked off her scaling ladder by a stone, but she quickly recovered and scrambled up the ladder, saying "Up, up, friends! The Lord has judged the English. Take heart, and the place is ours." She led her soldiers to victory once again. This time, another English commander, the Earl of Suffolk, was taken prisoner.

The French victory in the battle of Patay was a triumph of courage, luck, and speedy action. The English forces were lying in wait for Joan's army in a wooded area that offered good cover. The French commanders knew that their enemies would be looking out for them, and they were reluctant to move forward. Nevertheless, Joan encouraged them to continue onward, despite the danger. As the French carefully moved along their route, they startled a stag (a male deer) who plunged forward into the exact area where the English were hiding. As a result, the English soldiers were disturbed and called out with surprise. However, their shouts gave away their hiding place. Immediately the French charged into battle, and the English were so taken aback that they had no time to prepare their weapons or gather into fighting position. This was why they lost so many men. Of course, Joan's reputation was even further enhanced by this. As she was always guided to victory by her voices, she appeared to be invincible.

After Patay, it was time to go north to Reims itself. But first they needed to gather additional forces and equipment. Eleven days later, on June 29, Joan, the Dauphin, and the Coronation Army (as it was called) set off from Gien—a small town on the Loire River about 40 miles (65 km) west of Orléans. Reims was about 130 miles (210 km) to the northeast, and three towns lay along their route—Auxerre, Troyes, and Chalons. Because all this territory was occupied by the English and by their allies the Burgundians, the concern was always what kind of reception they would have on the way.

Fortunately, after three days of negotiations, Auxerre promised to obey the Dauphin, and the towns-people provided the army with food. Troyes, the next city, was going to be a difficult town to persuade. It was here that the French and English had signed a treaty disinheriting the Dauphin in favor of the king of England. From their camp outside the city, the Dauphin and Joan each sent letters in advance urging the citizens to come over to their side. In response, the citizens sent a Franciscan friar, Brother Richard, to see Joan and decide whether she truly was sent from God. Brother Richard came up to her cautiously, making a sign of the cross and sprinkling holy water. In response, she laughed and teasingly said, "Approach me boldly, I shall not fly away!" His report was favorable. However, the citizens of Troyes were still prepared to resist attack.

The Dauphin himself was filled with doubts about the wisdom of attacking Troyes. However, Joan told him confidently that she would take the town the next day. Her determination filled her army with courage. Just as she predicted, the citizens of Troyes simply caved in. On Sunday, July 10, they allowed the Dauphin to enter their city in triumph. Joan was beside him, carrying her standard.

By the time the Coronation Army reached Chalons, the final city on their way to Reims, all opposition had melted away. There, the citizens immediately welcomed the Dauphin with great warmth and joy. Joan experienced a special moment of happiness when she realized that her father and godfather had journeyed up from Domrémy to con-gratulate her on her spectacular successes. Not only had she relieved the siege of Orléans, but she had

This nineteenth-century statue of Joan of Arc shows what she looked like at the coronation of Charles VII. The coronation took place at Reims Cathedral, one of the largest cathedrals in all of France. Many French kings have been crowned in this cathedral.

also defeated the English in so many battles. Most important, she succeeded in bringing the Dauphin to the place where he would be crowned.

By this time, Reims itself had caught the mood of joyful welcoming. On the evening of July 16, Charles the Dauphin entered the town to great shouts of welcome by everyone. He had already met representatives from the city authorities who had come to declare their city's total support and obedience.

Reims Cathedral was quickly prepared. The very next day, July 17, 1429, the archbishop of Reims crowned the Dauphin (from that moment to be known as King Charles VII) and anointed him with the sacred oil. The ceremony lasted from nine in the morning until two o'clock in the afternoon. Joan stood beside the new king, wearing her white armor and carrying her personal banner. She was weeping tears of joy.

TROUBLES AHEAD FOR JOAN

Joan had arrived outside Orléans on April 29. Amazingly, in just over eleven weeks, she had accomplished what no one believed possible. Everything had happened just as the voices of St. Catherine and St. Margaret had foretold. Orléans had been rescued from the English, and many towns occupied by the English had surrendered. Furthermore, huge tracts of territory, which had formerly owed allegiance to the English king, had now swung over to acknowledge Charles VII as their lawful sovereign. Most important, the Dauphin had been given new confidence and regal authority when he was finally anointed king in Reims Cathedral.

It was quite astonishing to see a seventeen-year-old girl, who had fought battles against overwhelming odds, standing beside her newly crowned king. Joan was weeping for joy and holding her banner. It was not personal pride that moved her to tears, but the deep satisfaction that God's will had been done.

Naturally, she was anxious to follow up these triumphs with her final objective: to take Paris and restore Charles VII as the rightful king of France. At that time, the English king who ruled Paris was Henry VI of England, an eight-year-old boy, son of Henry V. However, it was really Henry V's brother, the Duke of Bedford, who ruled Paris and northern France.

The Duke of Bedford was extremely angry about this unforeseen coronation at Reims. He thought Joan was a witch. He also believed that witches should be burned. At that time, the usual punishment for those suspected of witchcraft was to be tied to a stake and burned alive.

DIFFICULTIES WITH THE KING AND HIS ADVISERS

Little did Joan realize that everything would soon become much more difficult.

This is an illuminated manuscript page from the *Bedford Book of Hours*. This image shows the Duke of Bedford praying before St. George, the patron saint of England. The duke later became regent of France when Henry V died.

This photograph shows the Château Sully-sur-Loire, where Joan of Arc met with the Duke of La Tremouille. The castle is a superb example of a medieval fortress.

Charles the Dauphin, who had become King Charles VII, was weak, lazy, naive, and indecisive. He always had to be persuaded to take any positive action. Unfortunately for Joan, after the coronation, he was far more preoccupied with making diplomatic bargains with his enemies the Burgundians than with

continuing the fight to regain more territory. If Charles had followed up the triumph of Reims with a determined attack on Paris, Joan would most probably have succeeded in capturing the city. Sadly for her, she became more and more disregarded at Charles's court, and the critical moment for action slipped by.

Another problem was that not all the French commanders were pleased with Joan's successes, because their own plans had often been ignored. Joan's bossy commands (which often urged them to take dangerous risks) were at times completely against their way of thinking. Chief among the Dauphin's military advisers was the Duke of La Tremouille, a hugely self-important but weak-willed man. His main policy at all times was to risk nothing. He resented a mere peasant girl being brought in to tell him how to run his armies. He was constantly at Charles's side, sneering at Joan's seemingly impossible plans.

But there was something else that made Joan uneasy at this time. She no longer heard her voices.

This is a portrait of Charles VII, circa 1450. By this time, he was calling himself Charles the Victorious. This painting is housed in the Musée de Louvre in Paris, France.

This must have upset her deeply. Joan found that she had to rely more and more on her own common sense. It meant that she was without the support and guidance of her saints. It was little wonder that with inaction and opposition at court, Joan's actions now appeared to lack the inspirational drive they had once had.

Joan's common sense told her that Paris must be taken, and she was constantly begging Charles to entrust her with this task. But the days and weeks went by, and Joan's frustrations must have become greater. On August 23, she simply took the law into her own hands. Accompanied by the Duke of Alençon and the Count of Vendôme, she led a small army to St. Denis, about 5 miles (8 km) north of the center of Paris. Charles had not ordered her to do so, but neither had he forbidden her. She left with no real plan of action. However, after she had inspected the defenses of Paris, she felt ready to write to Charles to request that he join her at once.

At this time, the king was concluding an armistice with the Duke of Burgundy that was to last until Christmas. This gave the duke the right to continue his alliance with the English. It even allowed him to defend Paris on behalf of the English against the French. This crazy agreement obviously

This is an illuminated manuscript illustration that shows Joan of Arc leading her troops into Paris to attack. Known as Lutetia (Lutece) in ancient times, Paris was conquered by Julius Caesar in 52 BC. Under the Romans and in the early Middle Ages, Paris was only of regional importance. The city's position as France's capital became established in AD 987.

made any further military action quite impossible for Joan.

Communications were slow, and for a while, Joan continued to make plans to attack Paris. Acting impulsively, she tried to storm one of the gates of the city. However, she only got as far as climbing a high bank on a surrounding moat. She was signaling for her soldiers to follow her, when an arrow hit her, piercing her between the coat of mail and the thigh piece. She fell to the ground, calling out to her men to carry on the attack without her. She lay on the ground until nightfall, but the attack on the gate was abandoned.

The Duke of Alençon and Joan received direct instructions from the king to stop their military actions. They were to return to the duke's temporary court at Gien, which was on the banks of the Loire. Such an order must have sickened Joan. But direct orders from the king had to be obeyed, especially since her voices were no longer guiding her.

These are the heraldic arms given to Joan of Arc's family at Christmas, 1429. On a blue background, there is a silver sword and a crown, with a fleur-de-lys on each side. Joan's family members were made nobles and given permission to take the name "du Lys." These gifts were accepted by Joan's brothers on the family's behalf. However, Joan refused them for herself. She said she asked for nothing except "good weapons, good horses, and money to pay the people where she lodged."

Thankfully, her leg wound healed quickly. But throughout the autumn of 1429, Joan remained at the royal court in Bourges, where she was bored. At Christmas, the king gave her a worthless, trivial present: the right for herself and her family to carry heraldic arms with the royal lilies of France, with the name "du Lys." He had given her neither money nor land. This gift (the only reward she was to be given) was of no practical value or help to her at all.

Spring came, and during Easter week of 1430, Joan's eagerness to attack Paris took over. By now, the truce between the French and the Burgundians had been long forgotten. Slipping away from La Tremouille's beautiful castle at Sully (where the king and his court were staying), Joan and a small company of soldiers moved to the town of Melun. Melun was about 24 miles (38 km) southeast of Paris. The inhabitants were eager to get rid of the English and Burgundians who were occupying their city. Because of this, Joan's French forces were treated as welcome liberators.

JOAN'S VOICES RETURN

Just as Joan entered Melun, her voices suddenly came to her again, this time with a powerful warning. She learned that she would be taken prisoner "before the feast of St. John [June 24]. Be not afraid," they said, "but take all things well, for God is with you." She begged to know the time of her capture and that she might be permitted to die at that hour.

This terrifying prophecy came true on May 23, 1430. Joan had decided to visit her friends in Compiègne, hoping to liberate them from the occupying Burgundians. Leading from the front and brilliantly dressed in red and gold, she entered the town. However, the governor was not willing to let a battle develop. He gave orders to raise the drawbridge. Although most of her companions escaped, Joan was trapped inside the city. Retreat was impossible. She was surrounded by Burgundians, dragged from her horse, and handed over to her captor, John of Luxembourg. It was very lucky for him. John of Luxembourg sold Joan for 10,000 crowns to the powerful Duke of Burgundy. The duke was delighted to have captured her at last.

JOAN IN CAPTIVITY

At first Joan's captors locked her up in the fortress of Beaulieu-en-Vermandois. After she tried to escape, she was taken to the Duke of Burgundy's castle of Beaurevoir in the woods between St. Quentin and Cambrai. This was about 60 miles (96 km) northwest of Rouen. For a while she was treated kindly by the lord of the castle and his family. However, she couldn't stand being held in captivity. When she learned that she was going to be handed over to the English, she made a spectacular second attempt to escape. This time, she leapt from a 60-foot (18 m) tower. Incredibly, she was uninjured. However, she was so stunned by the fall that she couldn't eat for days.

In fact, the voices of her saints had forbidden her to leap when she had told them she was tempted to do so. Afterward they forgave her for her foolishness and disobedience. Her voices were now speaking to her regularly. St. Catherine told her that Compiègne, which was occupied by the English, would be relieved "before Martinmas [November 11]." In fact, this happened in October.

In 1430, just before Christmas, Joan was taken from Beaurevoir to Rouen to face trial. Her judge was the bishop of Beauvais, Pierre Cauchon. He had been the head of the University of Paris. He had also taken a leading role in drawing up the Treaty of Troyes. In this treaty, England and France were placed under the single crown of England. Because of this, Cauchon was respected and trusted by the English and the Burgundians.

This is a representation of St. Catherine, one of the saints whose voices Joan claimed to have heard. Catherine was said to be a Christian girl who had defied the pagan Emperor Maxentius in the fourth century. His soldiers tried to crush her body on a wheel, but it broke. Nonetheless, she kept proclaiming her beliefs. Finally, she was beheaded.

Bishop Cauchon had his own reasons for hating Joan. As a friend of the English, he had been forced to escape from Reims when Joan had brought the Dauphin to be crowned there. Also, he had been obliged to escape from Beauvais when that town had decided to support Charles as king of France. It was also widely known that he wanted to become the archbishop of Reims. He hoped that he might gain this appointment if he made himself useful to the English in condemning Joan in her trial.

As soon as it was known that Joan had been captured, Cauchon wrote to the Duke of Burgundy. He demanded that she be handed over to him as a heretic—a person who holds beliefs contrary to the teachings of the church. He followed this up in July by writing directly to John of Luxembourg. However, it wasn't until November 21 that Joan was finally handed over to the English. This was after John of Luxembourg had negotiated the enormous sum of 10,000 crowns in payment for her.

Throughout the summer and autumn, Cauchon busied himself setting up the trial. He traveled widely, seeking out witnesses and gathering a large number of interrogators. These included representatives of the grand inquisitor of France (whose task it was to investigate heretics), priests, assessors, secretaries, lawyers, clerks, and doctors of theology who could thoroughly examine Joan's beliefs. The whole point of the trial was to prove Joan to be a heretic and enemy of the church. The most important person leading the trial was none other than the English king's uncle. Henry Beaufort was bishop of Winchester and cardinal of England. However, the brains and energy behind the trial belonged to Cauchon himself. And he seemed to be driven by hate.

The English, of course, were delighted that Joan had been captured. They were also pleased that a French ecclesiastical court was being used to put her on trial for heresy. Witchcraft was universally feared and hated. Also, if she were proved guilty of sorcery and magic, it would imply that the crowning of Charles at Reims had been invalid. To condemn Joan would make Charles guilty by association.

JOAN'S TRIAL BEGINS

Joan was being held in filthy and freezing conditions in the castle of Bouvreuil at Rouen. She was watched day and night by hostile English guards. At last, her long-awaited trial began in January 1431. It took place in the royal chapel of the castle at Rouen. Day after day, for weeks, Joan was questioned for hours

Dieu tout puissant createur du
monde universel fist et crea
tous les celestiens esperitz bon
et vertueux leur donnāt les
haulx dons de nature et de grace. Car
comme dit saint Augustin avecq la
noble nature quil leur bailla il les
doma aussi de vertu et grace. Mais
comme ilz eussent en leur premere in
stitucion receu de dieu voulente frāce

at a time on every conceivable matter relating to her lifestyle, beliefs, actions, and attitudes.

Her replies were always straightforward, filled with common sense, and often tinged with humor. She agreed to answer every question as truthfully as she could. Often, she managed to make her interrogators seem ridiculous. She was comforted by the fact that the voices of her saints were speaking to her daily. They were telling her that everything would turn out well if she remained courageous and outspoken.

Cauchon and his fellow judges questioned her about the Fairies' Tree in her early childhood. They tried to suggest that she was somehow involved in occult practices. "In what form did your angels appear to you?" she was asked. She replied that she was not permitted to answer. Joan did admit that St. Margaret and St. Catherine were wearing expensive-looking crowns. She also declared that she had God's permission to tell them this. Furthermore,

Pictured at left are witches and evil spirits in an illustration from a fifteenth-century Flemish manuscript that was a treatise on evil spirits and witchcraft. During Joan of Arc's time, people who were considered witches or warlocks (the male equivalent of a witch) were greatly feared. They were seriously persecuted. Often, these supposed witches were people who, in modern times, would be considered quirky or possibly mentally ill.

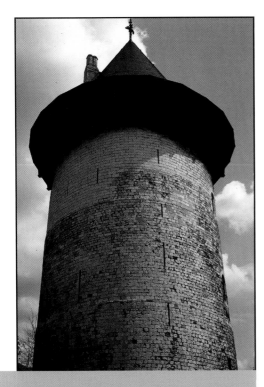

This tower at Rouen is the only surviving part of the castle where Joan was imprisoned and where her trial took place. It is known as Joan of Arc's Tower. However, although she must have passed through it as it was part of the castle's entrance, she was actually imprisoned in one of the castle's other towers.

she said they spoke "très bien et belle-ment" (very well and beautifully) in low, sweet tones.

Then, when one of her judges asked if St. Margaret spoke to her in English, Joan burst out, "Why should she, when she isn't on the English side!" When someone else asked her if St. Michael had appeared to her as a naked man, she sharply replied, "Why do you think God can't afford clothes for him?" There were smiles and laughter at this.

They also questioned her about her desperate leap from the tower at Beaurevoir. She admitted that she had been wrong to do this. After all, it had been forbidden by her voices. However, she defended her right to try to escape. Some of her replies were extremely shrewd, and it was difficult for her judges to find anything seriously wrong with her. However, there was one major sticking point that obviously meant a great deal to her as well as to the judges. It was the charge of wearing men's clothes, which was thought to be sinful. Cauchon was determined to make a big issue of this, but Joan was adamant that her saints' voices had commanded her to wear men's clothes. During her campaigns, it had been practical. The clothing had given her a military image and prevented her male companions from thinking of her as sexually attractive.

Week after week, the judges hurled questions at her. As Easter approached, they withdrew to Cauchon's house to consider the evidence. At first their findings (which were recorded by Jean d'Estivet, one of the court officials) consisted of no fewer than seventy articles of condemnation. Many of these were completely absurd or else nasty distortions of the truth. Joan was accused of possessing magic rings, of consulting with demons, and of living in a brothel when she was fifteen. She was even accused of casting spells at the Fairies' Tree. Some of these accusations were even too silly for the judges to accept. After further discussion, the final list was cut down from seventy points of accusation to twelve.

Above all, the crucial issue was still the matter of her voices. Were they really from God? Could she really prove this? And what if the church instructed her that she was deceiving herself? Should she continue to believe in her own judgment, or should she accept the teaching of the bishops and priests who told her she was wrong? This was the key question, and Joan was insistent in her response. She said she would maintain the truth of her voices even if she saw the stake before her and bundles of wood ready to burn her body.

Such stubbornness could produce only one result. Early in the morning on May 24, she was led to a spot outside the Abbey of St. Ouen in Rouen. The stake was already in place for her. The executioner was ready to light the fire.

The final scenes

As Joan was led to the stake, she passed an impressive scene outside the Abbey of St. Ouen. Three platforms had been built. The first one was for Bishop Cauchon and his fellow priests who had conducted the trial. Another platform was for the bishops and clergy from the area around Rouen. The third was for Cardinal Beaufort, uncle of the English king and bishop of Winchester, who represented the powers of both England and the pope.

The occasion began with a sermon condemning individuals who cut themselves off from the teachings of the church. When the preacher launched into a savage attack on the Dauphin, it was too much for Joan to bear. She shouted out in fury, "Don't talk about the king! He is the most noble of you all! If there is any fault, it is mine alone!" She was then asked again if she would withdraw her defiance of the church's teaching. In reply she asked if she could appeal to the pope himself. It was a final hope, but her request was immediately refused, with no reason given. To everyone's astonishment, Joan then panicked and gave in. Amid scenes of confusion, she signed a "confession" that had been quickly prepared for her:

> I, Joan, called the Maid, a miserable sinner . . .
> do confess that I have grievously sinned by
> claiming lyingly that I had revelations from
> God and his angels.

In her distress, she signed it all with a cross. She agreed to wear female dress and obey the church. Her will to resist had been broken. In an agonizing moment, she thought that perhaps her voices had been leading her to damnation.

The English authorities were severely disappointed as she was led away. However, Cauchon had made assurances that Joan would not escape. One of the judges calmed the enraged Earl of Warwick, telling him not to worry. He was certain they would get her convicted sooner or later.

Naturally, Joan expected to be pardoned and given her freedom. But when she returned to her prison cell, she learned the terrible truth. She would be expected to live for the rest of her life in prison, wearing female dress and praying constantly for forgiveness. The inquisitor's deputy and a number of her judges visited her in prison. They told her bluntly that if ever she went back on her word, the church would disown her completely. This would inevitably send her to hell.

This is the actual crucifix that Joan of Arc prayed before prior to her execution. The cross dates from the fifteenth century.

Joan was given women's clothing to wear. No one knows exactly what happened over the next few days. One possibility is that her jailers stole the clothes and forced her to change back into her own male clothing. It's more probable that she was simply determined to defy her judges, and this was her dramatic way of doing so. Certainly it was the excuse they were looking for, and they were enraged at her stubbornness. Cauchon summoned his forty-one assessors, and they unanimously decided to hand her over

This section of stained-glass window at the Cathedral of Orléans illustrates the execution of Joan of Arc. This is one of a series of ten impressive windows. Placed in the cathedral in 1895, the windows tell the story of Joan's life. Even today, the people of Orléans remember her.

immediately to the English secular authorities. It seemed clear to everyone that Joan was a heretic and was determined to return to her ways of wickedness. The church would have no more to do with her, except that she would be given the last sacrament.

THE MARKETPLACE AT ROUEN

Exactly one week after Joan was led to the stake outside the Abbey of St. Ouen, she was brought out of prison again. She was wearing a long penitential dress and a tall hat bearing the words, "Heretic. Relapsed. Apostate. Idolatress." The stake had been set high upon a huge pile of firewood in the middle of Rouen's old marketplace, where everyone would have a good view.

However, the scene was too terrible for many to watch. As Joan prayed for the last time, the crowd grew silent. She asked for a cross, and an Englishman made a rough little cross out of firewood for her to hold. Meanwhile, two young priests, Ysambard de la Pierre and Martin Ladvenu, managed to get a tall crucifix from a nearby church, and they pressed forward to hold it before her in her last moments. The executioner was given the sign to light the lowest bundles of firewood, and the flames soon spread. Ladvenu's crucifix would have been the last thing Joan saw as the smoke and flames engulfed her. She called out to her saints. She was heard to call out an anguished cry of "Jesus!" and then all was over.

Raking among the ashes afterward, the executioner found that her heart and entrails had not burned away. Since he had been given strict orders that no relics were to be left, he dutifully flung her last remains into the river Seine.

JOAN'S "REHABILITATION"

There must have been many who felt guilty and horrified by Joan's death. Even as the flames died down, people murmured, "We are lost! We have burned a saint!" The English authorities were glad to be rid of her, but their hold on France was now beginning to loosen. Over the next decades, they lost city after city as the French armies won them back. Also, they became less interested in France as English politics revolved around the internal struggles known as the Wars of the Roses.

A turning point came in 1435, when the Duke of Burgundy joined forces with Charles VII. By then, the English position had become hopeless. In 1450, Rouen itself became the last town in Normandy to fling out its English military occupants. By 1453, the English forces had been driven from France except for the channel port of Calais. It was to remain in English hands until 1558. At that time, the political link between France and England (begun by William the Conqueror) would be broken forever.

Throughout all this time, Charles VII had gained more importance and credibility. His ingratitude toward Joan and his complete indifference to her fate at the time of her imprisonment was inexcusable. By this point, he was calling himself Charles the Victorious. It was important to him that his coronation at Reims be recognized as valid. The English had always refused to accept this.

Obviously, in order to do this, it was necessary to resurrect the honor of Joan herself in some way. Therefore, when Joan's widowed mother Isabelette d'Arc wrote to the pope to ask for her daughter's good name to be reinstated, Charles eagerly supported a second trial. Its purpose would be to denounce the original judges and declare them corrupt.

The rehabilitation trial took six years to complete. Many of Joan's closest friends and companions, such as Jean de Metz and Bertrand de Poulengy, came to speak in her defense. Unfortunately, de Baudricourt had died. However, written evidence was provided by the Duke of Alençon and Count Dunois. Even the

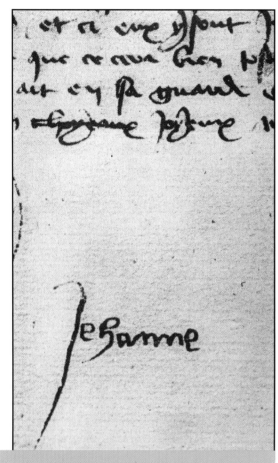

clerks who had taken down reports of what was said at the original trial, twenty-four years earlier, testified against Cauchon and the judges. Of course, the outcome of this trial was as predictable as the first had been. However, at the end of it Joan emerged as an honest heroine. On July 7, 1456, she was solemnly rehabilitated, and the sentence of excommunication against her was cancelled.

This is the signature of Joan of Arc. The youngest of five children born to Jacques and Isabelette, baby Joan was christened "Jehanne" (Joan in French) d'Arc. She referred to herself as Jeanne la Pucelle d'Orléans, the Maid of Orléans.

Over the centuries, the story of Joan, La Pucelle, or the Maid of Orléans, as she came to be called, has seized the imagination of artists, sculptors, and writers. She had always been seen as a heroine in the city of Orléans. Her memory is kept alive as the townsfolk annually commemorate their liberation from the English by her inspired leadership. However, it was not until the beginning of the twentieth century, in 1904, that her reputation grew to such an extent that the Catholic Church decided to declare her "venerable." In 1908, she was declared "blessed." Finally, in 1920, she was canonized to become Saint Joan, the patron saint of France.

As a historical figure, Joan is unique. Her influence on French history was immense. Her military successes helped to transform the morale of her fellow countrymen and thus pave the way to banishing the English forces from France. But she was not politically minded. She had not been schooled in philosophy, theology, or any intellectual subject. She couldn't even read or write. Her military skills were totally self-taught. Throughout her short life, she relied on nothing and no one except her own common sense and her mysterious voices.

All those who have studied the history of Joan of Arc have been astonished at her extraordinary life. Tourists and historians continue to visit the places associated with her in order to consider her life more deeply.

For almost five centuries, Winchester Cathedral in England has housed the sumptuous tomb of

Cardinal Beaufort, uncle of the English king and bishop of Winchester—the man who had overseen Joan's trial and personally witnessed her cruel death.

At last, on May 30, 1928, on the anniversary of Joan's death in 1421, an act of reconciliation took place in the cathedral. A statue of Joan, which shows her wearing her gleaming armor and famous sword, was unveiled in front of many important dignitaries, including the French ambassador. The statue faces Beaufort's tomb. At its base is a tiny fragment of stone from the dungeon in Rouen, where Joan spent her last agonizing days.

TIMELINE

1412 Birth of Joan of Arc at Domrémy.

1415 England defeats France at the Battle of Agincourt.

1421 Birth of King Henry VI of England.

1422 Death of Henry V of England and Charles VI of France. Henry VI is proclaimed the new king of England, and Henry V's brother, John, Duke of Bedford, is made regent (i.e. ruler) in France.

1428 Joan visits de Robert Baudricourt at the castle at Vaucouleurs. Beginning of the siege of Orléans.

1429 Joan visits de Baudricourt again in January and sets off to see the Dauphin at Chinon. In April she leaves Blois with an army to relieve the siege of Orléans and succeeds in doing this on May 8. She then captures many towns on the way to Reims, which surrenders on July 16. Charles VII is crowned the following day.

1430 May 23, Joan is captured at Compiègne.

1431 January 9, court assembles for Joan's trial at Rouen. May 19, Joan is condemned. May 24, Joan "gives in" to her judges at the church of St. Ouen in Rouen. May 27, Joan resumes dressing as a man. May 28, Joan is condemned as a "relapsed heretic." May 30, execution of Joan in the marketplace of Rouen.

1435 Death of the Duke of Bedford.

1436 Charles VII of France enters Paris in triumph.

1448 Rouen falls to the French, and over the next two years, the English are completely defeated. Only Calais remains in English hands.

1455 Joan's trial of rehabilitation.

1904 Joan is declared to be "venerable" by the Roman Catholic Church.

1908 Joan is declared to be "blessed."

1920 Joan is finally declared a saint.

GLOSSARY

apostate   One who abandons his or her religion and refuses to accept the authority of the church and its leaders.

armistice   An agreement to stop fighting. A truce.

Ascension Day   A special day in the church year, commemorating the moment when Jesus ascended into heaven after he rose from the dead.

blessed   A title given to those who are in the process of being canonized. It is the second stage in the process, following the title "venerable."

breach of promise   A legal term meaning that someone has broken his or her promise to marry.

Britanny   A territory in northwestern France, ruled by an independent duke during Joan of Arc's time.

canonize   To be officially declared a saint by the Roman Catholic Church. Joan of Arc was canonized on May 16, 1920. The anniversary of her death, May 30, is celebrated as her feast day. She is regarded as one of the two patron saints of France. She is also the patron saint of soldiers.

cardinal   The highest rank of priesthood in the Catholic Church.

Catherine   One of the saints who regularly "spoke" to Joan. She was cruelly martyred at about age twenty, in the fourth century, at Alexandria, Egypt. She is considered to be the patron saint of many groups, including young girls.

charismatic   Powerfully attractive to others. Many great leaders are charismatic to their followers.

confessor   A personal chaplain to someone of importance, who conducts religious services for his master or mistress and who hears their confessions.

coronation   The ceremony at which a monarch is crowned.

courtier   Someone who attends the king at his palace or castle. Some courtiers may be very high-ranking advisers; others might be servants.

crown   A golden coin, first minted in France in 1339, bearing a crown on one side.

dauphin   The title of the heirs to the throne of France. It is the French word for "dolphin," which was their traditional heraldic emblem.

decisive   Definitive or final.

ecclesiastical court   A court of law set up by church authorities.

fleur-de-lys   A heraldic emblem representing a lily on the official arms of France.

Infectious   Capable of spreading easily or of being contagious.

inquisitor   An official appointed to investigate cases of heresy.

Invincible   Unbeatable.

Margaret   One of the saints who regularly "spoke" to Joan. St. Margaret is the patron saint of women, nurses, and peasants. She is believed to have been martyred in the third or fourth century and was buried at Antioch (Antakya) in what is now Turkey.

Michael   The first vision Joan experienced was of the archangel Michael, who was believed by the church to be the captain general of the armies of heaven. Although Joan said that she saw him, she could never be persuaded to describe him, but she had no doubt in her mind that her vision was truly that of Saint Michael.

Normandy   A territory in northern France, held by the English at the time of Joan of Arc.

occult   Referring to supernatural or paranormal practices or happenings.

penitential dress   A rough gray garment worn by those who repent of their sins.

prophesied   Foretold. When someone foretells the future, he or she is said to have prophesied what will happen.

regent   Someone who rules a country for a king or queen who is still too young to do so.

rehabilitation The restoration of a person's good name and reputation.

relapse To return to a bad state of self. For example, a sinner who turned away from sin but came back to it would be relapsed.

page A young servant, often a boy, who ran errands for his master or mistress. In medieval times, pages often wore special clothes to show whose household they belonged to.

pucelle The French word for a virgin. Joan of Arc was popularly known as La Pucelle d'Orléans, or the Maid of Orléans.

sacrament The bread and wine taken at the Christian church service of Mass, or Holy Communion. The last sacrament is given to those about to die.

Salic Law A set of laws dating from the fifth century in France. Some of these laws prevented women from inheriting land and goods from their husbands. The Salic Law was also interpreted to argue that women and their descendants should not succeed to the French throne.

secular Not being connected to the church.

spellbound Mesmerized or completely fascinated by someone or something with remarkable qualities.

standard An identifying personal flag carried before military commanders in battle.

Standard-bearer   Someone who carries a "standard" or banner, often in battle but also on ceremonial occasions.

stronghold   A fortress or any place that is protected against attack.

theologian   Someone who studies religion and who is an expert in religious matters.

venerable   Worthy of reverence. It is a title given to those who are in the first stage of becoming canonized.

Wars of the Roses   The name given to the civil war in England in the fifteenth century, fought between two groups who used red or white roses as their emblems.

FOR MORE
INFORMATION

WEB SITES
Due to the changing nature of Internet links, the Rosen Publishing Group, Inc., has developed an online list of Web sites related to the subject of this book. This site is updated regularly. Please use this link to access the list:

http://www.rosenlinks.com/lema/joar

FOR FURTHER READING

Buchan, Alice. *Joan of Arc and the Recovery of France*. London: Hodder and Stoughton, Ltd., 1948.

Pernoud, Régine, Marie-Véronique Clin, and Jeremy Duquesnay Adams. *Joan of Arc: Her Story*. London: Palgrave Macmillan, 1999.

Shaw, Bernard. *Saint Joan*. London: Constable, 1924.

Steele, Philip. *The Medieval World*. London: Kingfisher, 2000.

BIBLIOGRAPHY

Barrett, W. P. *The Trial of Jeanne d'Arc*. London: George Routledge & Sons, 1931.

Pernoud, Régine. *Jeanne d'Arc*. Trans. Edward Hyams. London: Macdonald & Co., 1964.

Pernoud, Régine. *The Retrial of Joan of Arc—The Evidence at the Trial for Her Rehabilitation 1450–56*. Trans. J. M. Cohen. London: Methuen, 1955.

Smith, John Holland. *Joan of Arc*. London: Sidgwick & Jackson, 1973.

Twain, Mark. *What Is Man? and Other Essays of Mark Twain*. Freeport, NY: Books for Libraries Press, 1972.

INDEX

ABOUT THE AUTHOR

David Hilliam grew up in Salisbury and Winchester and was educated at both Oxford and Cambridge Universities. He has taught at schools in Canterbury, London, and Versailles, France. He is passionately interested in the British monarchy. His books include *Kings, Queens, Bones, and Bastards; Monarchs, Murders, and Mistresses;* and his latest, *Crown, Orb, and Sceptre,* which is an account of all the British royal coronations. At present he lives and works in Dorset, England.

CREDITS